Lucy Cowdery's

Spelling Rulebook

Lucy L Cowdery,
B.Ed. (Hons), M.Ed., AMBDA

TRTS Publishing

PO Box 1349, Wrexham, Wales. U.K. LL14 4ZA
Tel: 01978-840868 Fax: 01978 845715
email: books@trts.co.uk website: www.trts.co.uk

This publication is based on the Spelling Notebook,
copyright © 1987 TRTS Publishing, which was first published
as Book "F" of the "Teaching Reading Through Spelling
Programme" which is widely used in the U.K. to train
teachers of dyslexic pupils. Copies of these publications
are available from the Publishers.

First Edition   1998
Reprinted   2001

Published by:

       TRTS Publishing,
       PO Box 1349, Wrexham, Wales, U.K. LL14 4ZA
       Telephone 01978-840868
       Facsimile 014978-845715
       Email: books@trts.co.uk
       Website: www.trts.co.uk

       ISBN 1-900283-08-5

Printed in Great Britain by Watkiss Studios Limited, Bedfordshire.

Foreword

The Spelling Rulebook contains all the rules and generalisations of English spelling and is an indispensable reference book for teachers of English.

By using this book, an understanding of the spelling system of the English Language can be developed and made explicit. This will enable teachers to help all students of the English Language but particularly those who have an implicit processing difficulty.

The Spelling Rulebook was developed as part of the "Teaching Reading Through Spelling" programme (also known as The Kingston Programme) which is widely used in the UK to train teachers of dyslexic pupils. The book is used as an essential part of a psycholinguistic training programme which not only incorporates phonics but also articulation and speech training, analysis of the structure of the English Language, development of syntactic and semantic knowledge and the use of the historical roots of the language.

Some of the rules have been given in two forms. These are to be used according to the age and ability of the student and the individual teacher will be the best judge as to which version will best suit the needs of the students he or she teaches.

Early training emphasises the phonic principles which recur in English, thus encouraging the student to use, automatically, his or her own knowledge of phonics when reading and spelling phonically regular words. Later, the student learns to recognise the words with non-phonetic elements which make up only about 15% of all English.

Generalisations for the phonic spelling of sounds and words, syllable division rules, rules of affixing and plural rules complete the programme. These provide the student with much needed practice in linking sound to symbols and help him or her to focus attention on the structure of words.

Lucy Cowdery
B.Ed. (Hons), M.Ed., AMBDA

Lucy Cowdery is an expert in the field of Dyslexia and has used her spelling programme with great success, helping students of all ages with a variety of difficulties and levels of ability. She was trained by Kathleen Hickey and Jean Auger and headed the Kingston Reading Centre where the Spelling Rulebook evolved as a result of her work there. This work therefore is firmly grounded in practice. Lucy Cowdery has trained many teachers in the support of dyslexic students.

Contents

Contents

Contents

Contents

PART 3: SYLLABLE DIVISON RULES

PART 4: SUFFIXES AND PREFIXES

Contents

Part 1

Introduction

Linguistic Concepts

The following linguistic concepts are necessary for understanding the spelling rules:

1. **Differences between vowels and consonants.**

2. **Difference between short (˘) and long (¯) vowels.**

3. **What a syllable is.**

4. **Difference between closed and open syllables.**

5. **Parts of speech.**

All the rules and generalisations depend upon recognition of word patterns. It is essential that the student understands the following:

When looking for the pattern in a word ALWAYS START WITH THE VERY FIRST VOWEL IN THE WORD and put v for vowel above it. Move from the first vowel to the last vowel in the word writing v for vowel or c for consonant above each letter.

e.g.

vccv	vcv	vccv	vcv	vcc	vc
letter	student	kidnap	bacon	bell	run

Sound Pictures

A letter underlined indicates <u>the name</u> of that letter:

Thus: *<u>a</u>*   *<u>c</u>*   *<u>v</u>*   etc.

Letters in brackets *( )* indicate <u>the sound</u> or sounds which a particular letter or letters make.

Thus: *<u>a</u> = (ă) (ā) (ŏ) (är) (ŭ)*

These are called **SOUND PICTURES**

A sound picture is a visual representation of what is heard. The brackets *( )* represent the 'ears' and what is inside the brackets is the sound or sounds heard.

Note: A full list of diacritical markings is given on page 172

<u>SPELLING FROM SOUND PICTURES</u>:

1. Some words are spelled exactly as they sound.

    (dŏg) - *<u>dog</u>*   *(kĭd)* - *<u>kid</u>*   *(hē)* - *<u>he</u>*

2. Double consonants are pronounced once, and do not therefore appear in sound pictures.

    (bĕl) - *<u>bell</u>*   *(mŭf)* - *<u>muff</u>*   *(lăs)* - *<u>lass</u>*

Sound Pictures

3. **_C_** has no sound of its own and appears in sound pictures as **(k)** or **(s)**.

    (kăt) - **_cat_**   *(sĭn'dēr)* - **_cinder_**

4. Silent letters do not appear in sound pictures.

    (hăv) - **_have_**   *(nē)* - **_knee_**   *(nōm)* - **_gnome_**

5. Sound pictures help a student to realise that words are not always spelled as they sound.

    (wŏz) - **_was_**   *(flī)* - **_fly_**   *(lŭv)* - **_love_**

6. Sound pictures are an aid to a student's awareness of spelling rules and a help to the teacher in as much as the student can see which rules and generalisations have been assimilated and which need to be taught or revised.

The Alphabet

A B C D E F G

H I J K L M N

O P Q R S T U

V W X Y Z

a b c d e f g

h i j k l m n

o p q r s t u

v w x y z

The Alphabet

There are 26 letters in the alphabet

There are 5 vowels

a *e* *i* *o* *u*

There are 21 consonants

b *c* *d* *f* *g* *h* *j* *k*

l *m* *n* *p* *q* *r* *s* *t*

n *w* *x* *y* *z*

The letter *y* may be either a vowel or a consonant depending upon its position in a word.

Vowels and Their Sounds

There are 5 vowels in the alphabet.
They are   **_a_**   **_e_**   **_i_**   **_o_**   **_u_**

Sometimes the vowels are short. Short vowels have a breve (˘) over them.

ănt	**ĕgg**	**ĭndian**	**ŏrange**	**ŭmbrella**
(ă)	*(ĕ)*	*(ĭ)*	*(ŏ)*	*(ŭ)*

Short vowels cannot say their names. They are like babies and have a cradle (˘) over them.

Sometimes the vowels are long. When they are long, they say their names. Long vowels have a macron (¯) over them.

ācorn	**ēqual**	**īron**	**ōpen**	**ūniform**
(ā)	*(ē)*	*(ī)*	*(ō)*	*(ū)*

Long vowels have long lines over them. (¯)

The Four Quartiles of the Alphabet

The four quartiles of the alphabet correspond to the four quarters of the 'Oxford Concise Dictionary'.

A   B   C   D

E   F   G   H   I   J   K   L   M

N   O   P   Q   R

S   T   U   V   W   X   Y   Z

NOTE:
The first letter of each quartile should be given a clue-word. This will help you to remember them.

e.g.

Apples

Eggs

Nuts

Sausages

Part 2

Basewords

The Word, I

Any time the letter _**i**_ stands alone, it is a word and must be written with a capital letter.

The word *I* means _**myself**_.

Final (l) ll, l

ll

1. If there is only one vowel in the word use *ll*.

   e.g. *ball*   *well*   *ill*   *doll*   *gull*

l

2. If there is another consonant helping to protect the vowel, use *l*.

   e.g. *girl*   *curl*   *whirl*   *hurl*

If there are two or more vowels in the word use *l*.

e.g.   *wheel*   *goal*   *camel*   *easel*   *bevel*

THINK:
Is there only one vowel?
Is it unprotected?
If there is only one vowel and it is unprotected, use *ll*.

EXCEPTIONS:
nil, *pal*.

Final (f) ff, f

ff

If there is only one vowel in the word and it ends with the sound (f) use **ff**.
e.g. **stăff clĭff ŏff mŭff**

f

1. If there is another consonant helping to protect the vowel, use **f**.
   e.g. **scarf elf turf shelf wolf**

2. If there are two or more vowels in a word, use **f**.
   e.g. **leaf chief belief roof beef**

THINK:
Is the vowel short?
Is it unprotected?
If it is short and unprotected, use **ff**.

EXCEPTION: *if*

NOTE: *(ŏv) of*

Final (s)   _ss_

_ss_

If there is only one short vowel in a word
and it ends with the sound **(s)** use **_ss_**.
e.g. **_măss_**   **_lĕss_**   **_hĭss_**   **_tŏss_**   **_fŭss_**

EXCEPTIONS:
gas   _yes_   _his_   _us_   _plus_   _bus_   _thus_

NOTE:
A single **_s_** at the end of a word denotes
the plural (more than one thing).
Otherwise, a single **_s_** at the end of a
word has the sound **(z)**.
e.g. **_is_**   **_his_**   **_as_**   **_has_**   **_was_**

L.F.S. Rule

At the end of a one syllable word, straight after one short vowel, the letters $\underline{l}$, $\underline{f}$ and $\underline{s}$ are doubled.

e.g.   **bĕll**   **cŭff**   **mĭss**

EXCEPTIONS:

nil   **if**   **gas**   **this**   **bus**   **thus**
pal   **of (ŏv)**   **yes**   **us**   **plus**

REMEMBER:

If a word ends in a single $\underline{s}$ it has the sound **(z)**. e.g. **is** **his** **as** **has** **was** Otherwise, a single $\underline{s}$ denotes the plural, (more than one thing).

Vowel Sounds in Syllables

One vowel at the end of an open syllable is long.

$h\bar{e}$ $sh\bar{e}$ $m\bar{y}$ $s\bar{o}$ $g\bar{o}$ $fl\bar{u}$

A vowel in a closed syllable is short.

$h\breve{e}dge$ $sh\breve{e}d$ $m\breve{i}ll$ $g\breve{y}m$ $s\breve{o}b$ $c\breve{u}t$

Short Vowel Pattern (S.V.P.)

hĕn is a closed syllable.

Closed syllables have short vowel sounds and the vowel is closed in by one or more consonants.

When a short vowel sound is heard in the first syllable of a two syllable word, it must be followed by more than one consonant before the next vowel in the word.

This is the short vowel pattern: vccv

   vowel + consonant + consonant + vowel

   v c c v   v c c v
   napkin   _upset_

REMEMBER:
When looking for the pattern in a word, always start with the first vowel. You disregard all consonants before that first vowel.

Short Vowel Pattern (S.V.P.)

"Rabbit Words"

In a two syllable word, when only one consonant sound is heard after a short vowel sound in the first syllable, that consonant is usually doubled.

e.g. We hear (*răb'ĭt*)
but we spell the word **ra<u>bb</u>it**.

We hear (*tĕn'ĭs*)
but we spell the word **te<u>nn</u>is**.

The consonant must be doubled in order to maintain the short vowel pattern, vccv.

<table>
<tr><td align="center">v c|c v</td><td align="center">v c|c v</td></tr>
<tr><td align="center">*rabbit*</td><td align="center">*tennis*</td></tr>
</table>

REMEMBER:
The short vowel pattern is <u>vccv</u>

28

Short Vowel Pattern (S.V.P.)

The short vowel pattern is:

vowel + consonant + consonant + vowel

$$\text{vccv}$$
(vccv) as in *năpkin*

When a short vowel sound is heard in the
first syllable of a multi-syllable word,
it must be followed by more than one
consonant before the next vowel in the
word. e.g.

vccv · · · · · · vccv · · · · · · vccv

jumping · · · *mended* · · · *limpid*

When only one consonant sound is heard
after a short vowel sound in the first
syllable of a multisyllable word, that
consonant must be doubled before the next
vowel. e.g.

vccv · · · · vccv · · · · · vccv · · · · · · vccv

rabbit · · · *sullen* · · · *running* · · · *hopped*

REMEMBER: VCCV

The Sounds of, <u>Y</u>

---

1. **CONSONANT** <u>y</u> sounding *(y)*

<u>Y</u> only acts as a consonant when it is the first letter in a word.

e.g. *you*   *yes*   *yet*   *year*   *yellow*

---

2. **VOWEL** <u>y</u> sounding *(ĭ)* and *(ī)*.
When <u>y</u> is anywhere else in a word it is a vowel and takes the sounds of vowel <u>i</u>.

<u>Y</u> *(ĭ)*   *gym*   *pygmy*   *puppy*
<u>Y</u> *(ī)*   *type*   *tyre*   *sky*   *try*

NOTE:
We often give final <u>y</u> the sound *(ē)*.
<u>mummy</u>.

REMEMBER:
<u>e</u> is always silent at the end of words. If you **hear** the *(ē)* sound use <u>y</u>.
<u>store</u> but *<u>story</u>*.

Spelling Final (ī) *y* , *ie*

English words do not end in the letter *i*.

y

In a one syllable word with the sound *(ī)* at the end, choose *y* after two consonants.

cry *dry* *fly* *fry* *pry* *sky* *shy* *why*

ie

Choose *ie* after one consonant.

die *lie* *pie* *tie* *vie*

EXCEPTIONS:
my *by*

The Sounds of <u>C</u>

The letter <u>c</u> has no sound of its own.

<u>c</u> has the *(s)* sound when it is followed by
<u>e</u>, <u>i</u> and <u>y</u>.

e.g. ***cell***   ***celery***   ***city***   ***citric***   ***cycle***

We call this <u>the soft sound of</u> <u>c</u>.

<u>c</u> has the *(k)* sound everywhere else.

e.g. ***cap***   ***cot***   ***cub***   ***cling***   ***crest***   ***act***   ***cry***

We call this <u>the hard sound of</u> <u>c</u>.

Spelling Initial and Medial (k)

$\underline{k}$

At the beginning, or in the middle, of a word use $\underline{k}$ before $\underline{e}$, $\underline{i}$ and $\underline{y}$.

kettle   **_king_**   **_sky_**   **_askew_**   **_akin_**   **_kennel_**

$\underline{c}$

Use $\underline{c}$ everywhere else.

cat   **_cod_**   **_cup_**   **_cling_**   **_crisp_**   **_act_**   **_decay_**

$\underline{ck}$

Use $\underline{ck}$ in multisyllable words to retain the short vowel pattern (VCCV).

	VCCV	VCCV	VCCV
e.g.	**_packet_**	**_cricket_**	**_pocket_**

REMEMBER:
$\underline{k}$ can never follow a short vowel.

EXCEPTIONS:

kangaroo, **_kayak_** - not English words.

Spelling Final (k)

ck

Use **ck** at the end of one syllable words immediately after a short vowel.

e.g. **băck** **pĕck** **lĭck** **blŏck** **dŭck**

ke

Use **ke** at the end of one syllable words immediately after a long vowel.

e.g. **bāke** **Pēke** **līke** **blōke** **dūke**

k

1. Use **k** after a consonant.

   bank **desk** **link** **clonk** **milk** **lark**

2. Use **k** after a vowel digraph.

   book **seek** **leak** **soak** **creak** **week**

Spelling Final (k)

c

1. Use **ic** to spell the **(ĭk)** sound at the end of multisyllable words.

   Atlantic   **hectic**   **picnic**   **Pacific**

---

2. Words ending in **c** must add **k** before suffixes beginning with **e, i** and **y** in order to keep **c** hard.

   e.g.   **panicked**   **panicking**   **panicky**

que

A few words derived from the French language end in **(k)** spelled **que**.

antique   **grotesque**   **clique**   **oblique**   **unique**
pique.

NOTE:

i before **que** has the sound **(ē)**.

Spelling Initial and Medial (sk)

sk

Use **sk** at the beginning, or in the middle, of a word before **e, i** and **y**.

e.g. **skeleton**　**skin**　**sky**　**basket**

sc

Use **sc** everywhere else.

scar　**scout**　**scuttle**　**describe**

EXCEPTIONS:

skull (link with **skeleton**).
skate　**skunk**

Spelling Final (sk)

Always use **_sk_** at the end of words.

e.g. **_mask_** **_desk_** **_risk_** **_tusk_** **_cask_**

EXCEPTIONS:
disc *mollusc*

NOTE:
With the advent of the computer, we now
have *__floppy__* *__disk__*.

Spelling Initial and Medial (j)

g

Use **g** before **e, i** and **y** (except for the syllable **ject**).

e.g. **gem**   **gipsy**   **gym**   **engine**   **angel**

j

Use **j** everywhere else.

e.g. **jam**   **job**   **jug**   **jumper**   **jade**

ject

Remember the syllable **ject**. It is very common.

e.g. **subject**   **object**   **adjective**   **injection**

NOTE: **j** is never doubled.

SOME COMMON EXCEPTIONS:
jeans   jet   Jew   jewel   jelly   jersey jealous.

Spelling Final (j) d<u>ge</u>, <u>ge</u>.

d<u>ge</u>

Use **d<u>ge</u>** at the end of one syllable words straight after one short vowel.

e.g.　**b<u>ădge</u>**　**l<u>ĕdge</u>**　**r<u>ĭdge</u>**　**l<u>ŏdge</u>**　**dr<u>ŭdge</u>**

<u>ge</u>

Use **<u>ge</u>** everywhere else.

e.g.　**<u>cage</u>**　**<u>huge</u>**　**<u>barge</u>**　**<u>hinge</u>**　**<u>rage</u>**

<u>age</u>

Final **(ĭj)** in words of two or more syllables is spelled **<u>age</u>**.

e.g.　**<u>message</u>**　**<u>cabbage</u>**　**<u>luggage</u>**

NOTE:
English words never end in the letter **j**.

Spelling Final (d) and (t)

(d) <u>d</u>   **(d)** <u>ed</u>   (past tense suffix).
(t) <u>t</u>   **(t)** <u>ed</u>   (past tense suffix).

When the sounds **(d)** and **(t)** are heard at the end of a word think, *"Is it the past tense of a verb?"* (i.e. *"Is it an action that has already taken place?"*) If so, the **(d)** and **(t)** sounds will be spelled with <u>ed</u>.

e.g. *play - <u>played</u>   oil - <u>oiled</u>   kick - <u>kicked</u>*

Everywhere else the **(d)** and **(t)** sounds will be spelled with <u>d</u> and <u>t</u>.

e.g.   <u>bad</u>   <u>lad</u>   <u>fed</u>   <u>hat</u>   <u>not</u>   <u>sit</u>

BE CAREFUL.

When there is a change of vowel sound between the present and past tense of a verb, the **(d)** and **(t)** sounds will be spelled with <u>d</u> and <u>t</u>.

e.g.   <u>sĕll - sōld</u>   <u>fēed - fĕd</u>   <u>behōld - behĕld</u>
       <u>slēep - slĕpt</u>   <u>kēep - kĕpt</u>   <u>wēep - wĕpt</u>

<u>a</u> sounding (ŏ)

<u>**a**</u> often has the sound **(ŏ)** when it follows
<u>**w**</u>, <u>**wh**</u>, and <u>**qu**</u>.

e.g. <u>**was**</u>   <u>**wash**</u>   <u>**wand**</u>   <u>**swan**</u>
      <u>**what**</u>   <u>**quads**</u>   <u>**squash**</u>

The Letter V

No English word ends in the letter **_v_**.
A silent **_e_** must be added.

e.g. **_have_**   **_give_**   **_live_**   **_save_**

The letter **_v_** is never doubled in English words.

e.g. **_gravel_**   **_devil_**   **_snivel_**   **_hovel_**   **_level_**

ove

The sound **_(ŭv)_** is spelled **_ove_**.

e.g. **_above_**   **_dove_**   **_love_**   **_glove_**

NOTE:
The words **_spiv_** and **_navvy_** are now included in some dictionaries.

Spelling (z) z̲ or s̲

1. Use **z̲** at the beginning of words.

   e.g.   *z̲oo*   *z̲ebra*   *z̲ig-z̲ag*

2. Use **s̲** in other positions in a word.

   e.g.   *is̲*   *has̲*   *ros̲e*   *mis̲er*   *advis̲e*

REMEMBER:

1. A single **s̲** at the end of a word usually denotes a plural or has the sound *(z)*.

2. **s̲** between two vowels usually has the sound *(z)*

Spelling (kw) <u>qu</u>.

The letter *q* must always be followed by the letter <u>*u*</u>. Together, they make the multiple consonant sound *(kw)*.

e.g.   <u>*quack*</u>   <u>*queen*</u>   <u>*quick*</u>   <u>*question*</u>

NOTE:

When the letter <u>*u*</u> is with *q* it is not counted as a vowel. It is only there to give *q* a sound. So, in the word quick there is only one vowel and that is (ĭ) <u>*i*</u>.

all   _well_   _full_   _till_

The words **_all_**, **_well_**, **_full_**, and **_till_** drop an
_l_ when they are added to another word.

REASON:
They are no longer one syllable words.

e.g.   _all_ +   _ways_   =   _always_
     well +   _come_   =   _welcome_
     help +   _full_   =   _helpful_
     _un_   +   _till_   =   _until_
     full +   _fill_   =   _fulfil_

The Long Vowel Pattern (L.V.P.)

$h\bar{e}$ is an <u>open syllable</u>.
Open syllables have long vowel sounds and
the vowel is left open.

When a long vowel sound is heard in the
first syllable of a multisyllable word,
there is <u>only one consonant</u> before the
next vowel in the word.

This is the long vowel pattern :-

vowel + consonant + vowel   (<u>VCV</u>)

$\overset{\text{V}|\text{CV}}{b\bar{a}|con}$ $\overset{\text{V}|\text{CV}}{\bar{e}|vil}$ $\overset{\text{V}|\text{CV}}{\bar{i}|ron}$ $\overset{\text{V}|\text{CV}}{c\bar{o}|lon}$ $\overset{\text{V}|\text{CV}}{d\bar{u}|ty}$

<u>REMEMBER</u>:
The long vowel pattern is <u>VCV</u>

e.g $\overset{\text{VCV}}{\underline{\textbf{\textit{hate}}}}$ $\overset{\text{VCV}}{\underline{\textbf{\textit{hating}}}}$ $\overset{\text{VCV}}{\underline{\textbf{\textit{hated}}}}$ $\overset{\text{VCV}}{\underline{\textbf{\textit{hateful}}}}$

Vowel + Consonant + _e_ (V-e)

1. A silent _e_ after one consonant opens up
   the syllable and makes the preceding
   vowel long.

   e.g. _mӑn_   _māne_
   sĭt   _sīte_

2. **V - _e_** is the regular spelling of long
   vowels in final closed syllables.

   e.g. _hāte_   _dictāte_   _athlēte_   _concrēte_
   fīve   _combīne_   _hōme_   _condōle_
   crūde   _dispūte_

NOTE:

Remember that _e_ is always silent at the
end of words. If you hear the sound (_ē_)
use the letter _y_.

e.g.   _store_ but _story_.

Spelling Final (s) <u>ss</u> <u>ce</u> <u>se</u>

<u>ss</u>

Use <u>ss</u> at the end of one syllable words straight after a short vowel.

e.g. <u>**măss**</u> <u>**lĕss**</u> <u>**hĭss**</u> <u>**tŏss**</u> <u>**fŭss**</u>

<u>ce</u>

Use <u>ce</u> at the end of one syllable words after a long vowel sound.

e.g. <u>*plāce*</u> <u>*plāice*</u> <u>*flēece*</u> <u>*īce*</u> <u>*pūce*</u>

<u>BUT NOTE</u>: <u>*cāse*</u> <u>*chāse*</u> <u>*bāse*</u> <u>*dōse*</u> <u>*close*</u>

<u>se</u>

Use <u>se</u> after <u>**ou**</u>, <u>**oo**</u> and <u>**ea**</u>.

e.g. <u>**house**</u> <u>**mouse**</u> <u>**goose**</u> <u>**loose**</u> <u>**grease**</u> <u>**lease**</u>

<u>BUT NOTE</u>: <u>*peace*</u>

<u>REMEMBER</u>:
A single <u>**s**</u> usually denotes a plural or has the sound *(z)*. <u>**has**</u>

48

Spelling Final (z) zz se ze

zz

> Use **zz** at the end of one syllable words straight after a short vowel.
>
> e.g.   **jăzz**   **fĭzz**   **bŭzz**

se

> Use **se** after a long vowel sound.
> {Except after long vowel **(ā)**}.
>
> e.g.   **chēese**   **rīse**   **nōse**   **fūse**   **chōose**
>
> **BUT NOTE:**   *size*

ze

> Use **ze** usually after long vowel **(ā)**.
>
> e.g.   **hāze**   **dāze**   **māze**   **māize**   **grāze**

REMEMBER:

s between two vowels has the sound **(z)**.
A single **s** at the end of words usually denotes a plural or has the sound **(z)**.

e.g.   *is*   *his*   *as*   *has*   *was*

Spelling Final (īz) *ise* *ize*

ise

Use *ise* to spell the final syllable (īz) when it is part of the baseword.

e.g. *advise*   *devise*   *exercise*   *franchise*

NOTE:*s* between two vowels has the sound (z)

ize

ize is a suffix meaning to make. It is added to a baseword.

e.g. *magnetize*   *popularize*   *dramatize*

REMEMBER:

1. When a final syllable is taken off a word, only part of the word is left.

    e.g. *advise - ise = adv*

2. When a suffix is taken off a word, a whole word is left.

    e.g. *magnetize - ize = magnet*

Vowels Combined With r

When a single vowel is followed by a single **r** in the same syllable, the sound of the vowel is regularly changed.

In accented syllables:
ar is regularly pronounced *(är)* as in *car*.
or is regularly pronounced *(ôr)* as in *fork*.
er, **ur** and **ir** are regularly pronounced
as in *term   nurse   girl*

After **w**, **or** is regularly pronounced *(ûr)* as in *word*.

In unaccented syllables:
all vowel combinations with **r** are usually pronounced *(ẽr)*.

e.g. *hammer (ẽr)   doctor (ẽr)   collar (ẽr)*

When a vowel is followed by 2 **r**'s the vowel regularly has its short sound.

e.g. *ărrow   tĕrror   mĭrror   bŏrrow   bŭrrow*

When to use _er_ in words

1. **_er_** is most common at the end of words.

   e.g. **_hammer_**   **_sister_**   **_winter_**   **_summer_**

2. **_er_** is common in the middle of multisyllable words.

   e.g. **_general_**   **_certificate_**   **_advertise_**   **_generate_**

3. **_er_** is the most common spelling of the sound **_(ûr)_** after the letter **_p_**.

   e.g. **_perch_**   **_perhaps_**   **_permit_**   **_person_**   **_perfume_**

4. **_er_** is not usually used in the middle of one syllable words. Here are a few you should know.

   fern   **_term_**   **_germ_**   **_nerve_**   **_serve_**   **_verse_**

5. **_er_** is hardly ever used at the beginning of words.

   err   **_ermine_**   **_ern_**   **_erst_**

When to use _er_ in words

6. **_ser_** is rare in an initial syllable. Here are the words you should know.

serf   **_serge_**   **_sermon_**   **_servant_**   **_serve_**   **_serpent_**

REMEMBER:
If in doubt, use **_er_** at the end of words and in the middle of multisyllable words.

*When to use **ur** in words*

1. **ur** is common in the middle of one syllable words.

   e.g. *curl*   *turn*   *curse*   *purse*   *curve*   *purl*

2. **ur** is always used for the days of the week.

   e.g.   *Thursday*   *Saturday*

3. **ur** is usually used for words connected with hospital.

   e.g. *surgeon*   *nurse*   *hurt*   *burn*   *burst*

4. **cur** is the most common spelling of the sound *(kûr)*.

   e.g. *curtain*   *curfew*   *cursive*   *curtsy*

5. In initial syllables the sound *(sûr)* is most frequently spelled **sur**.

   e.g. *surface*   *surname*   *surprise*   *surly*

When to use __ur__ in words

6. __ur__ is very unusual at the end of words.
   e.g. __cur__ __fur__ (of an animal), __spur__

7. Not many words start with *(ûr)* __ur__.
   e.g. __urban__   __urchin__   __urge__   __urgent__
   __urgency__   __urn__ (a vase).

8. There are about 25 words where the
   sound *(pûr)* is spelled __pur__. (The most
   common spelling being __per__).
   e.g. __purchase__   __purgatory__   __purl__   __purple__
   __purport__   __purpose__   __purr__   __purse__
   __pursue__   __pursuit__   __purvey__

__REMEMBER__:

If in doubt, use __ur__ in the middle and __er__
at the end.

e.g.   __murder__,   __curler__

When to use *ir* in words

1. *ir* is used for numbers.
   e.g. *first*   *third*   *thirteen*   *thirty*

2. *ir* is used for words connected with girls.
   e.g.
   Girls wear *skirts* and *shirts*.

3. The most common use of *ir* is in words which come from the Latin word circus which means a circle. Use *cir* for the *(sûr)* sound if the word has to do with a circle.
   e.g. *circular*   *circumference*   *circulate*

NOTE:

er, *ur* and *ir* have the same sound.
If in doubt, use *er* at the end of a word, *ur* in the middle and *ir* for girls, numbers and circles.

e.g. *Murder in the first degree.*

When to use <u>or</u> to spell the sound (ûr)

Always use or after **<u>w</u>** to spell the sound **(wûr)**.

e.g. **<u>word</u>   <u>world</u>   <u>worm</u>   <u>work</u>**

BUT NOTE: *<u>worn</u>*

Other Spellings of Accented (ûr)

ear

1. The **(ûr)** sound at the beginning of words is usually spelled **ear**.

   e.g. **earl   early   earn   earnest   earth**

2. Learn the others as a word family.

   **heard   learn   pearl   rehearse
   search   yearn**

our

The following words have **our** spelling the **(ûr)** sound. Learn them as a word family.

**adjourn   journal   journey
scourge   sojourn**

Spelling Unaccented (ẽr)

er

1. ***er*** is the most common spelling of the ***(ẽr)*** sound in the middle of multi-syllable words.
   e.g. ***general   certificate   thermometer***

2. When ***er*** is the final syllable in a word, it is usually <u>a suffix meaning</u>:

   a) <u>The one who</u>, e.g. ***teacher   learner   baker***

   b) <u>That which</u>, e.g. ***rocker   folder.***

   c) <u>Comparative of adjectives and adverbs.</u> Here it means <u>more</u> and is used when comparing <u>two things</u>.
      e.g. ***I am tall but he is taller.***
      He is fast but she is faster.

   d) An inhabitant:
      e.g. ***Londoner   islander***

3. Many words ending in ***er*** are short, simple words of everyday living.
   e.g. ***winter   sister***

Spelling Unaccented (ẽr)

or

1. ***or*** is a Latin suffix meaning, <u>the one</u> <u>who</u> or <u>that which</u>.
   It is used at the end of words when the root ends in ***ct, it, ate,*** or ***ess.***

   e.g.   ***actor***   ***tractor***   ***doctor***   ***editor***
             creditor   ***indicator***   ***possessor***

2. These common nouns ending ***or*** should be learned as a word family.

anchor	***author***	***error***	***major***	***minor***
mirror	***governor***	***sailor***	***tailor***	***terror***

Spelling Unaccented (ẽr)

ar

1. Use **ar** in adjectives when it means *like*.
   e.g. *circular*   *angular*   *singular*.

2. Use **ar** at the end of words, usually after **ll**.
   e.g. *collar*   *dollar*   *cellar*   *pillar*

3. Use **ar** in a final syllable before **d**.
   e.g. *orchard*   *coward*   *custard*   *wizard*

4. **ar** is also a suffix meaning:

   a)   the one who
        e.g. *scholar*   *beggar*   *pedlar*

   b)   that which
        e.g. *hangar*

NOTE ALSO:
grammar   *calendar*   *mortar*

Spelling Unaccented (ĕr)

re

re is used in words relating to measurement.

e.g. **acre**   **metre**   **litre**   **centimetre**

NOTE ALSO:
massacre   **mediocre**   **ogre**

ure

Learn these words as a word family.

injure   **leisure**   **measure**   **pressure**
seizure   **treasure**

our

These words should also be learned as a word family.

ardour   **armour**   **clamour**   **colour**
favour   **labour**   **odour.**

Spelling (ôr)

or

1. Use **_or_** at the beginning, in the middle and at the end of words.

   e.g. ***orb*** ***orbit*** ***fork*** ***scorn*** ***for*** ***nor***

ar

2. Use **_ar_** after **_w_, _wh_** and **_qu_**.
   e.g. ***war*** ***warm*** ***wharf*** ***quarter*** ***quartz***

a + *l* + *consonant*

3. When **_a_** is followed by **_l_** plus another consonant it has the sound **_(ôr)_**.

   e.g. ***all*** ***talk*** ***bald*** ***almost***

EXCEPTIONS:
alp ***scalp*** ***shall*** ***talc***

Spelling (ôrt)

aught

> 1. There are only nine words in which the _(ôrt)_ sound is spelled _aught_.
>
> The _fraught_ father _caught_ his _naughty_ little _daughter_ and _taught_ her not to be so proud and _haughty_.
>
> ALSO: _aught_ (which means anything),
> _naught_
> _slaughter_

ought

> 2. Use _ought_ to spell the _(ôrt)_ sound, unless the word is one of the nine _aught_ words.
>
>   e.g. _ought_ (expressing duty),
> _bought_
> _brought_
> _thought_
> _fought_.

Spelling the Sound (är) *ar* *a*

ar

> Use *ar* at the end of words and before one consonant. e.g.
>
> *bar* *car* *far* *star* *jar* *tar* *bark*
> *cart* *start* *market* *lark*

a

> Use *a* to spell the (*är*) sound before two consonants.
> e.g.
> *pass* *path* *father* *staff* *fast*

EXCEPTIONS:

"The *harsh* man led the *march* beneath the *arch* across the *marsh* and down to the *larch* tree." *starch*.

Notice that the exceptions end in *sh*, *ch*.

NOTE:
This rule does not apply in areas where a broad (*ă*) is used. e.g. *băth*

Consonant Digraphs

A digraph is composed of two letters pronounced as one sound.

_ch_	-	_chair_	_(ch)_
_ch_	-	_choir_	_(k)_ Greek
_ch_	-	_chef_	_(sh)_ French
_ph_	-	_photograph_	_(f)_ Greek
_sh_	-	_ship_	_(sh)_
_th_	-	_thimble_	_(th)_ unvoiced
_th_	-	_that_	_(th)_ voiced
_wh_	-	_whistle_	_(hw)_

NOTE:

Remember the difference between a blend and a digraph:

Blend:

The sound of both letters is heard.
e.g. *cl, cr, pl, pr, sl, sw.*

Digraph:

Only one sound is heard.

Spelling (ch) _tch_ _ch_

tch

1. Use **_tch_** at the end of one syllable words straight after a short vowel.
   e.g. **_cătch_** **_fĕtch_** **_wĭtch_** **_blŏtch_** **_hŭtch_**

2. **_tch_** is used in words of more than one syllable to protect a short vowel.
   e.g. **_hatchet_** **_stretcher_** **_kitchen_** **_satchel_**

_ch_

Use **_ch_** everywhere else.
e,g, **_chat_** **_chest_** **_chin_** **_chop_** **_chuck_**
screech **_teach_** **_larch_** **_lunch_**

EXCEPTIONS:

rich **_which_** **_much_** **_such_** **_attach_** **_bachelor_**
detach **_duchess_** **_ostrich_** **_sandwich_**

Consonant Digraph   ch   ph

ch (k)

ch is the regular spelling of the **(k)** sound in words derived from the Greek Language; most of these words are medical, scientific or technical.

The most widely used are:

Christ,   Christmas,   Christian,   ache, stomach,   chemist,   chemical,   school, scholar,   scheme,   monarch,   orchestra,   choir, chorus,   chord,   echo,   orchid,   anchor, archive,   chaos,   character,   charisma, chloride.

ph (f)

ph is not a regular spelling for **(f)** but should always be considered as the first choice for **(f)** in spelling words connected with medicine, science and scholastic works from the Greek Language.

sulphur   camphor   lymph   physics, photograph   telephone   alphabet nymph   phrase

Spelling Long Vowel Sounds

Spelling long vowel sounds in multisyllable words:

A long vowel sound at the end of an open syllable is spelled with a single vowel.

e.g. _ā'pron_ _ē'qual_ _tī'ger_ _hō'ly_ _stū'pid_

NOTE:
Apart from a few simple words, _**be, he, me, she, we, go, no, so,**_ this type of syllable will always be found in words of more than one syllable.

Vowel Digraphs and Diphthongs

A vowel digraph is a combination of two vowels in one syllable having only one sound. In a digraph, one of the vowels will retain one of its sounds.

> *"When two vowels go walking,*
> *The first one does the talking.*
> *It will usually say its name".*

A diphthong is a blend of two vowels in one syllable. Neither vowel retains either of its sounds but forms a completely new sound. There are only four diphthongs in English and they are:

oil   _toy_   _out_   c_ow_

Vowel Digraphs and Diphthongs

ai	train	(ā)	ie	priest	(ē)
ay	tray	(ā)	ie	pie	(ī)
au	saucer	(au)	oa	boat	(ō)
aw	claw	(au)	oe	toe	(ō)
ee	tree	(ē)	oo	moon	(ōō)
ea	easel	(ē)	oo	book	(ŏŏ)
ea	head	(ĕ)	ou	out	(ou)
ea	steak	(ā)	ou	soup	(ōō)
ei	ceiling	(ē)	ow	cow	(ou)
ei	reindeer	(ā)	ow	snow	(ō)
ey	key	(ē)	ou	oil	(oi)
ey	obey	(ā)	oy	toy	(oi)
eu	Europe	(ū)	ue	argue	(ū)
ew	few	(ū)	ue	clue	(ōō)
			ui	fruit	(ōō)

NOTE:

ow can be a digraph, e.g. snow (ō)

ow can be a diphthong, e.g. cow (ou)

The Regular Spellings of (ā)

a

1. Use *a* at the end of an open syllable.

   e.g. *ā'corn*   *bā'con*   *relā'tion*   *cā'ble*

a-e

2. Use *a - e* in one syllable words which end in a consonant sound.

   e.g. *gate*   *made*   *sale*   *came*   *safe*

3. Use *a - e* in the final closed syllable of multisyllable words.

   e.g. *compensate*   *delegate*
        forsake   *lemonade*

ay

4. Use *ay* at the end of words.

   e.g. *day*   *play*   *dismay*   *relay*   *array*

Other Spellings of (ā)

ai

1. Use **ai** in the middle of one syllable words and in the final syllable of multisyllable words before the letters **d**, **l**, **n**, **r** and **t**.

   e.g. **maid** **tail** **train** **lair** **bait** **afraid**
   prevail **compalin** **despair** **portrait**

ea

2. There are only four words where **ea** spells **(ā)**

   break **great** **steak** **yea**

Great waves **break** on the shores of **Great** Britain. **Yea**! This **steak** is **great** to eat.

Other Spellings of (ā)

ei

3. There are not many words in which *ei* spells *(ā)*.

   deign   reign   reindeer   skein   veil

eigh

4. Learn these as a word family.

   eight   eighteen   eighty   freight neighbour   weigh

ey

5. Learn these as a word family.

   They, who obey, convey the prey to their masters.

The Regular Spellings of (ē)

e

Use **_e_** at the end of an open syllable.

e.g. **_mē_**   **_ē'qual_**   **_bē'tween_**   **_rē'tail_**

ee

1. Use **_ee_** in the middle of one-syllable words.

   e.g. **_feet_**   **_deed_**   **_greed_**   **_queen_**   **_meek_**

2. Use **_ee_** at the end of words.

   e.g. **_tree_**   **_free_**   **_degree_**   **_committee_**

e - e

Use **_e - e_** in the final closed syllable of multisyllable words.

e.g. **_athlete_**   **_convene_**   **_recede_**   **_obsolete_**

Other Spellings of (ē)

ea

---

ea is the second choice for **(ē)** in the middle of one-syllable words.

a. Words spelled with **ea** are usually homophones for words spelled with **ee**.

e.g. _meat_ , _meet_   _bean_, _been_
    beach , _beech_   _read_, _reed_
    peal, _peel_   _seam_, _seem_

b. Most words connected with eating spell the **(ē)** sound **ea**.

e.g. _eat_   _meal_   _tea_   _meat_   _feast_   _veal_
    bean   _pea_   _cream_   _wheat_   _yeast_

---

ei

Use **ei** after the letter **c**.
e.g. _ceiling_   _conceit_   _receipt_   _receive._

Other Spellings of ($\bar{e}$)

ie

Put *i* before *e* (except after *c*) when the sound is *($\bar{e}$)*

e.g. *piece*   *field*   *chief*   *yield*   *niece*

These words are best learned by grouping them in word family sentences.

e.g. *Wield a shield and they'll yield the field. The niece of the priest believes grief should be brief.*

The Regular Spellings of (ī)

_i_

1. Use _i_ at the end of an open syllable.
   e.g. _ī'ris_   _clī'mate_   _fī'nal_   _ī'cicle_

_i - e_

2. Use _i - e_ in one syllable words which end in a consonant sound.
   e.g. _five_   _time_   _ride_   _site_   _nine_

3. Use _i - e_ in the final closed syllable of multisyllable words.
   e.g. _derive_   _invite_   _coincide_

_y_

4. Use _y_ at the end of words.
   e.g. _cry_   _sky_   _rectify_   _multiply_

Other Spellings of (ī)

ie

1. Use *ie* at the end of words after one consonant.

    e.g. *die   lie   pie   tie   vie*

EXCEPTIONS: *by, my, bye, dye, rye.*

y

2. Use *y* in an opened accented syllable in Greek derived words.

    e.g. *cy'clone   py'thon   cy'cle*

y - e

3. Use *y - e* in final closed syllables in Greek derived words.

    e.g. *type   tyre   style*

Other Spellings of (ī)

igh

4. Learn as a word family.

high	*nigh*	*sigh*	*thigh*
fight	*light*	*might*	*night*
right	*sight*	*tight*	

NOTE:
Apart from the first four words, they all
end in *t*.

ei

5. There are not many words in which *ei*
   spells *(ī)*. Learn them as a word family.

   either   *neither*   *eider*   *height*   *sleight*

The Regular Spellings of (ō)

o

> 1. Use **o** at the end of an open syllable.
>   e.g. *sō* *ō'pen* *pō'ny* *rō'dent*

o-e

> 2. Use **o - e** in one syllable words which
>   end in a consonant sound.
>   e.g. *rode* *bone* *rope* *note*

> 3. Use **o - e** in the final closed syllable
>   of multisyllable words.
>   e.g. *explode* *disclose* *remote*

ow

> 4. Use **ow** at the end of words.
>   e.g. *snow* *grow* *throw* *blow*

Other Spellings of (ō)

oa

Use **oa** at the beginning of one syllable words.

e.g. **oak**   **oat**   **oath**   **oast**

Use **oa** in the middle of one syllable words. It is your second choice. (The first choice is **o-e**).

e.g. **boat**   **road**   **coast**   **coal**

ow

Use **ow** in the middle of one syllable words which end in a single **l** or **n**.

e.g. **bowl**   **grown**

oe

Use **oe** at the end of words after one consonant.

e.g. **doe**   **foe**   **roe**   **hoe**   **woe**

Other Spellings of (ō)

ou

ou (ō) is found in the middle of a few words. Learn them as a word family.

e.g. **soul**   **shoulder**   **boulder**   **mould**   **moult**

ough

Learn these as a word family.

though   **although**   **dough**

The Regular Spellings of (ū)

u

1. Use **u** at the end of an open syllable.
   e.g. **ū'nicorn   mū'sic   cū'pid   lū'pin**

u - e

2. Use **u - e** in one syllable words which end in a consonant sound.
   e.g. **cube   rude   rule   tune   mute**

3. Use **u - e** in the final closed syllable of multisyllable words.
   e.g. **compute   dissolute   execute**

ue

4. Use **ue** at the end of multisyllable words.
   e.g. **tissue   continue   rescue   avenue**

ew

5. Use **ew** at end of one syllable words.
   e.g. **crew   dew   flew   grew   hew   Jew**.

EXCEPTIONS: *blue, clue, cue, due, glue, hue, rue, sue, true.*

Other Spellings of ($\bar{u}$)

eu

Use *eu* in Greek derived words.

e.g. *Europe*   *feudal*   *pneumonia*

Spelling (ou) _ou_ _ow_.

_ou_

Use _ou_ at the beginning or in the middle of a word.

e.g. _out_   _ground_   _house_   _loud_

_ow_

Use _ow_ at the end of a word and when the (_ou_) sound is followed by a single _l_, _n_ or _er_.

e.g.
how	_cow_	_now_
howl	_prowl_	_owl_
crown	_town_	_brown_
flower	_shower_	_tower_

Spelling (au) _au_ _aw_

_au_

Use _au_ at the beginning or in the middle of a word.

e.g. _August_   _autumn_   _clause_   _haunt_

_aw_

Use _aw_ at the end of a word and when followed by a single _l_ or _n_.

e.g. _paw_   _claw_   _straw_   _jaw_   _law_
     crawl   _drawl_   _shawl_   _brawl_
     lawn   _fawn_   _dawn_   _prawn_

Spelling *al* (aul)

al (aul)

In one syllable words, an **a** followed by **l** is regularly pronounced **(aul)**.

SPELLING HELP:
(aul) is regularly spelled **al** or **all** in one syllable words.

e.g.   **bald**   **always**   **tall**   **ball**

Spelling (oi) _oi_ _oy_

_oi_

Use _oi_ at the beginning or in the middle
of a word.
e.g. _oil_   _coin_   _joint_   _spoil_

_oy_

Use _oy_ at the end of words.
e.g. _boy_   _toy_   _employ_   _destroy_

EXCEPTIONS:
The _loyal_ subject made a _voyage_ to find
oysters for his _royal_ master.

Rule for _ie_ and _ei_

1. If the sound is _(ē)_ use _i_ before _e_
   except after _c_.

   e.g. **chief**   **brief**   **relieve**   **belief**
   but
   ceiling   **receipt**   **receive**   **deceit**

2. If the sound is _(ā)_ put the letters the
   other way, _ei_.
   e.g. **weigh**   **neighbour**   **rein**   **vein**

EXCEPTIONS:

_"Neither leisured foreigner seized the weird
height."_

_"Either pay the forfeit or your heifer will be
thrown in the weir where there is a surfeit of
water."_

Spelling Final (ŭs)

1. **<u>us</u>** is a noun ending.

   e.g. ***crocus***   ***bonus***   ***virus***   ***circus***

2. **<u>ous</u>** is an adjective ending.

   e.g. ***nervous***   ***dangerous***   ***generous***

3. If the word has a ***(sh)*** sound before the ***(ŭs)*** use **<u>ious</u>**.

   e.g. ***malicious***   ***fictitious***   ***vicious***.

<u>NOTE</u>:

<u>contagious</u>   ***<u>religious</u>***
<u>porpoise</u>   ***<u>tortoise</u>***

<u>REMEMBER</u>:
A noun is a naming word.
An adjective is a describing word.

Scribal _o_ sounding (ŭ)

Scribal **_o_** has the sound **(ŭ)**.
It is used to spell the **(ŭ)** sound before
_m_, **_n_** and **_v_**.

e.g.   **_some_**   **_stomach_**   **_woman_**
       son   **_won_**   **_London_**
       love   **_glove_**   **_above_**

Stable Final Syllables

ble	nimble	age	cabbage
ckle	buckle	ate	certificate
cle	cubicle	ain	bargain
dle	puddle	ice	practice
fle	rifle	ile	fragile
gle	bugle	ine	engine
kle	ankle	ise	promise
ple	apple	ite	definite
stle	whistle	ive	active
tle	battle	ique	unique
zle	puzzle	------	
		tion	dictation
able	durable	sion	mansion
ible	forcible	sion	television
------		ssion	mission
dure	procedure	cian	magician
ture	picture	------	
------		tious	ambitious
ary	secretary	cious	malicious
ery	misery	ceous	curvaceous
ory	factory	tial	partial
ant	vacant	cial	facial
ance	variance	sial	controversial
ancy	vacancy	tient	patient
ent	frequent	cient	deficient
ence	audience	sient	transient
ency	urgency	------	

Stable Final Syllables

A stable final syllable forms part of the baseword; it is not usually accented.

1. When spelling words with stable final syllables, <u>listen for the vowel sound in the first syllable</u>. If it is short, close the syllable with the consonant you hear and then add the stable final syllable.
   e.g.

   nŏb + *ble* = *nobble*   Closed syllable
                                   Short vowel

   ăc + *tion* = *action*   Closed syllable
                                   Short vowel

2. If the vowel is long, leave the syllable open and then add the stable final syllable.
   e.g.

   nō + *ble* = *noble*   Open syllable
                                   Long vowel

   stā + *tion* = *station*   Open syllable
                                   Long vowel

Stable Final Syllables

stle

1. **_stle_ _(s'l)_** is regular for spelling.
   The **_t_** is silent.
   e.g. **_whistle_**   **_thistle_**   **_nestle_**   **_wrestle_**

   NOTE:
   The exceptions, **_muscle_**   **_mussel_**   **_tassel_**

zle

2. **_zle_ _(z'l)_** is regular for spelling.
   e.g. **_dazzle_**   **_sizzle_**   **_nozzle_**   **_puzzle_**

fle, ful

3. **_fle_ _(f'l)_** is a final stable syllable and
   forms part of the baseword.
   e.g. **_raffle_**   **_rifle_**   **_snaffle_**   **_shuffle_**

   ful _(f'l)_ is a suffix meaning 'full of'
   so can be taken off to leave a
   baseword.
   e.g. _cup + ful_ = **_cupful_**
        hope + ful = **_hopeful_**

Stable Final Syllable (k'l)

ckle

1. Use **ckle** straight after a short vowel in a two syllable word.

   e.g. **tackle** **freckle** **tickle** **cockle** **buckle**

cle

2. Use **cle** at the end of words of three or more syllables.

   e.g. **barnacle** **cubicle** **pinnacle** **chronicle**

NOTE:

The exceptions, **circle** **cycle** **treacle** **uncle**

kle

3. Use **kle** at the end of two syllable words after a vowel + consonant.

   e.g. **twinkle** **ankle** **sparkle** **crinkle**

Stable Final Syllable (k'l)

cal

cal is an adjective ending.

e.g. **nautical**   **tropical**   **musical**

cle

cle is always a noun ending.

e.g. **article**   **vehicle**   **circle**   **uncle**

REMEMBER:

A **noun** is a naming word.
An **adjective** is a describing word.

Stable Final Syllables -*le* -*el* -*al*

-*le*

1. When you hear the *(l)* sound at the end of a multisyllable word, use *le* if the letter before the *(l)* sound has a stick or a tail.

   e.g. **bubble**   **cradle**   **tickle**   **raffle**
        apple   **puzzle**   **toggle**   **tipple**

-*el*

2. If the letter before the *(l)* sound has no stick or tail, use -*el*.

   e.g. **tunnel**   **barrel**   **towel**   **travel**   **novel**

-*al*

3. If there is a whole word before the *(l)* sound, use *al*. -*al* is a suffix meaning to do with.

   e.g. **musical**   **political**   **electrical**

REMEMBER:

Never double *v*.

Stable Final Syllables -*le* -*el* -*al*

le

le is the most common spelling of the *(l)* sound at the end of multisyllable words.

e.g. **bubble   saddle   rifle   bugle   angle**

-*el*

1. Use *el* to keep *c* and *g* soft.

   e.g. **cancel   parcel   angel**

2. Use *el* if the letter before the *(l)* sound has no stick or tail.

   e.g. **tunnel   camel   towel   travel   barrel**

-*al*

1. Use *al* for adjectives.

   e.g. **central   local   egal   total**

2. Use *al* when there is a whole word before *(l)*.

   e.g. **musical   electrical   seasonal.**

Stable Final Syllables

Note these homophones:

meddle	*peddle*	*idle*	*bridle*	*principle*
medal	*pedal*	*idol*	*bridal*	*principal*

Homophones are words that sound the same but, they are not spelled the same and they do not have the same meaning.

The following words are irregular:

couple	*double*	*trouble*	*people*
treadle	*treble*	*triple*	
carol	*petrol*	*pistol*	*symbol*

Stable Final Syllables

ble + _ity_

Words ending in **_ble_** do not add **_ity_** in the usual manner; the **_ble_** becomes **_bil_** before **_ity_** and is always accented.

e.g. **_desirable_**   **_desirability_**
     reliable   **_reliability_**

cle and _gle_ + _cular, gular_

The endings **_cle_** and **_gle_** change their spellings to **_cular_** and **_gular_** when forming adjectives (describing words).

e.g. **_circle_**   **_circular_**
     angle   **_angular_**

Generalization: (shŭn)

tion

1. Use **tion** if the baseword ends in the sound **(t)** spelled **t** or **te**.
   e.g.
   distract - **distraction**   **act** - **action**
   dictate - **dictation**   **vacate** - **vacation**

2. Use **tion** immediately after short vowel **(ĭ)**.
   e.g. **condĭ tion**   **ambĭ tion**   **ignĭ tion**

3. Use **tion** if the **(shŭn)** sound comes after a long vowel sound.
   e.g. **accusātion**   **complētion**   **lōtion**
   institution

NOTE:
tion is the most common spelling of the **(shŭn)** sound.

Generalization: (shŭn)

sion

1. Use **sion** when the baseword ends in the sound **(s)** spelled **se**.

   e.g. **averse** - **aversion**
   diverse - **diversion**

2. Use **sion** when the companion word, a verb, ends in **nd**, **ge**, **vert** and **pel**

   e.g. **nd**   **comprehend, comprehension**
   ge   **emerge, emersion**
   vert   **convert, conversion**
   pel   **propel, propulsion**

NOTE:
The **(ĕ)** in **pel** changes to **(ŭ)** when **sion** is added.
e.g. **compĕl**   **compŭlsion**

Generalization: (shŭn)

ssion

1. Use **ssion** when the baseword ends in **ss**.
   e.g. *possess* - *possession*
   depress - *depression*

2. Use **ssion** when the companion verb ends in the Latin root **mit**, **ceed** or **cede**.

   e.g. *mit*   -   *admit*   *admission*
       ceed   -   *succeed*   *succession*
       cede   -   *concede*   *concession*

cian

Use **cian** when referring to people.

e.g. the magic man - *magician*.

REMEMBER:
If the baseword ends in **ic** the **(shŭn)** sound will be spelled **cian**. Take the **m** from **man** and put **i** in its place.

   electric man - *electrician*

Spelling *(zhŭn)*

sion

There is only one spelling of the *(zhŭn)* sound and that is *sion*.
e.g. *television, conclusion, explosion, erosion.*

REMEMBER:

sion has the sound *(zhŭn)* when it comes directly after a vowel.
e.g. *seclusion   provision*

sion has the sound *(shŭn)* when it comes directly after a consonant.
e.g. *tension   diversion*

Generalization: _cious_   _tious_

cious

> 1. **_cious_** is the most common way of spelling
> the sound **_(shŭs)_**.
> e.g.   **_precious_**   **_officious_**   **_delicious_**

tious

> 2. If you can find a companion word ending
> in **_(shŭn)_** **_tion_**, use **_tious_**.
> e.g. _fic**tion**_   _ficti**tious**_
>   _cau**tion**_   _cau**tious**_

NOTE:
suspicion - suspicious
consience - conscientious

Spelling Final (n) in Multisyllable Words

_an_

1. Use **_an_** for a person or a nationality.

   e.g. **_American_**   **_Parisian_**   **_artisan_**

_en_

2. Use **_en_** everywhere else.

   e.g. **_blacken_**   **_christen_**   **_hasten_**   **_lighten_**

NOTE:

_en_ is a suffix meaning made of or to make.

e.g. a golden ring is made of gold.
     to darken means to make dark.

Generalization: _ant_

ant - suffix forming adjectives
ent - suffix forming adjectives

ant

1. Use _ant_ if there is a companion word ending in _ātion_.
   e.g. _domination; dominant_
   variation; variant

2. Use _ant_ to keep _c_ and _g_ hard.
   e.g. _significant; elegant_

3. _ant_ is usually used for nouns meaning persons.
   e.g. _tenant_   _lieutenant_   _occupant_

EXCEPTIONS:
superintendent   _president_   _resident_
parent   _student_

Generalization: _ent_

ent

1. Use _**ent**_ to keep _c_ and _g_ soft.
   e.g. _**innocent**_   _**intelligent**_

2. Always use _**ent**_ after _**qu**_.
   e.g. _**frequent**_   _**eloquent**_

3. Use _**ent**_ for the _**escent**_ group of words.
   e.g. _**adolescent**_   _**convalescent**_

4. Use _**ent**_ when the root word contains
   _i_ or _e_.
   e.g. _**sufficient**_   _**proficient**_   _**convenient**_
        **obedient**

5. Use _**ent**_ after the Latin roots - _**fer, sist,**_
   **cur, haer, spond, min.**
   e.g. _**different**_   _**persistent**_   _**recurrent**_
        **inherent**   _**despondent**_   _**prominent**_

NOTE:
The Latin root _**haer**_ has lost the _a_ in
English usage.
e.g. _**adhere**_   _**cohere**_

Generalization: *ance* *ence* *ense*

ance -noun suffix meaning <u>state</u> or <u>act of</u>.
ence -noun suffix meaning <u>state</u> or <u>act of</u>.
ense -part of a baseword.

ance

1. Use **ance** if there is a companion word ending in **ā̄tion**.
   e.g. *domin**ation**; domin**ance***
   *vari**ation**; vari**ance***

2. Use **ance** to keep **c** and **g** hard.
   e.g. *signifi**cance** ele**gance***

3. Use **ance** to turn a verb into a noun.
   e.g. (verb) **appear**; (noun) **appearance**

4. Generally when the baseword contains a **o** or **u**, use **ance**.
   e.g. *b**al**ance perf**or**mance ab**un**dance*

110

Generalization: *ance* *ence* *ense*

ence

1. Use *ence* when the companion word ends in *escent*.
   e.g. *adolescent; adolescence*
   convalescent; convalescence

2. Use *ence* to keep *c* and *g* soft.
   e.g. *innocence* *intelligence*

3. Use *ence* always after *qu*.
   e.g. *eloquence* *frequence*

4. Generally when the baseword contains *i* or *e*, use *ence*.
   e.g. *audience* *experience* *difference*

5. Use *ence* after the Latin root *fer*. (carry, bear).
   e.g. *conference* *reference* *deference*

NOTE:
There is one exception, *sufferance*

Generalization: _ance_ _ence_ _ense_

ence

6. Use ence after the Latin root **_sist_**, (stand).
   e.g. **_subsistence_**   **_persistence_**

   NOTE: The exceptions:
   desistance   **_assistance_**   **_resistance_**

7. Use **_ence_** after the Latin root **_cur_** (run)
   e.g. **_occurrence_**   **_recurrence_**

8. Use **_ence_** after the Latin root **_haer_** {**_her_**}, (stick).
   e.g. **_adherence_**   **_coherence_**

9. Use **_ence_** after the Latin root **_spond_**, (promise).
   e.g. **_correspondence_**   **_respondence_**

10. Use **_ence_** after the Latin root **_min_** (jut).
    e.g. **_prominence_**   **_imminence_**

Generalization: *ance* *ence* *ense*

ense

1. ***ense*** is not a suffix. It forms the baseword.

   e.g. ***dense*** ***sense*** ***nonsense*** ***tense*** ***intense*** ***expense*** ***dispense*** ***suspense***

   NOTE:
   The exceptions, ***fence*** ***hence*** ***pence***

Generalization: _ancy_ _ency_

ancy

Use **_ancy_** to keep **_c_** and **_g_** hard.

e.g.
vacancy
  {**_c_** says **_(k)_**, need **_ancy_** to keep it hard}
arrogancy
  {**_g_** says **_(g)_**, need **_ancy_** to keep it hard}

ency

Use **_ency_** to keep **_c_** and **_g_** soft.

e.g.
decency
  {**_c_** says **_(s)_**, need **_ency_** to keep it soft}

urgency
  {**_g_** says **_(j)_**, need **_ency_** to keep it soft}

NOTE ALSO:
.... _ancy_	.... _ency_
infancy	_potency_
brilliancy	_frequency_
constancy	_presidency_
hesitancy	
malignancy	

Generalization: _ary_ _ery_ _ory_

ary

1. **_ary_** is the most common spelling of the
   sound **_(ĕr ĭ)_**.
   It is used for adjectives (describing
   words).
   e.g. **_momentary_**   **_ordinary_**   **_culinary_**

2. When it refers to people, **_ary_** is a noun
   ending. **_ary_** means <u>the one who</u>.
   e.g.
   secretary - the one who can keep secrets.
   visionary - the one who has visions.

ery

Use **_ery_** when the word refers to
occupation.
e.g. **_nursery_**   **_bakery_**   **_pottery_**   **_gunnery_**

ory

Because it follows **_t_** or **_s_**, **_ory_** is usually
easy to hear.
e.g. **_factory_**   **_explanatory_**   **_sensory_**   **_compulsory_**

Generalization: _able_ _ible_

able

1. We usually use **_able_** after a whole word.
   e.g. **_readable_** **_comfortable_** **_washable_**

2. We use **_able_** when the baseword ends in silent **_e_**.
   e.g. **_believe_** - **_believable_**
   move - **_movable_**

3. We use **_able_** to keep **_c_** and **_g_** hard.
   e.g. **_communicable_** **_navigable_**

ible

1. Use **_ible_** for words which are not complete without this ending.
   e.g. **_incredible_** **_horrible_** **_possible_**

2. We use **_ible_** to keep **_c_** and **_g_** soft.
   e.g. **_forcible_** **_reducible_** **_eligible_** **_legible_**

Generalization: _able_ _ible_

able   adjective suffix meaning _able_
          or _capable_.

ible   adjective suffix meaning _able_.

able

1. Use able if there is a companion word
   ending in _ation_
   e.g. _duration;_   _durable_
        variation;   _variable_

2. Use _able_ to keep _c_ and _g_ hard.
   e.g. _communicable_   _navigable_

3. Use _able_ to turn a verb or noun into an
   adjective.
   e.g. _move_ (verb) _movable_ (adjective)
        comfort (noun) _comfortable_ (adjective)

Generalization: _able_ _ible_

ible

1. Use _ible_ if there is a companion word
    ending in _tion_ or _sion_.

    e.g. _destruction_ - _destructible_
    accession - _accessible_

---

2. Use _ible_ to keep _c_ and _g_ soft.
    e.g. _forcible_ _reducible_ _eligible_ _legible_

NOTE: It is important that you think of
the _ation_ or _tion_ and _sion_ companion word
first.

Final Syllables   -*ist*   -*est*

The endings -*ist* and -*est* are similar in sound but remember:

1. The ending -*ist* is a Greek suffix which forms nouns. The suffix *ist* means "one skilled in or one who believes in".
   e.g. *dentist   typist   defeatist   pacifist*

2. The ending -*est* forms adjectives in the superlative degree.
   e.g. *tiniest   reddest   biggest   ripest*

REMEMBER:

A noun is a naming word.
An adjective is a describing word.

-*est* means 'the most' and is used when comparing three or more things.

Final Syllables -*ice* -*ine* -*ite* -*ive*

In words of more than one syllable, endings beginning with **i** often have the short vowel sound (ĭ) despite the silent **e** at the end of the words.

1. -*ice* (ĭs)
   office   **service**   **justice**   **practice**   **novice**

2. -*ine* (ĭn)
   engine   **doctrine**   **famine**   **discipline**

3. -*ite* (ĭt)
   granite   **opposite**   **favourite**   **definite**

4. -*ive* (ĭv)
   active   **captive**   **fugitive**   **massive**

-_ceed_   -_sede_   -_cede_

-_ceed_

ceed is used in only three words:
  exceed, _succeed_, _proceed_

-_sede_

sede is only used in the word, _supersede_

-_cede_

cede is used everywhere else, even in procedure.
  concede, _intercede_, _precede_

Part 3

Syllable
Division
Rules

Syllables

A syllable is a beat.
Every syllable has a <u>vowel sound</u> in it.
Words are made up of syllables.

One syllable words have <u>one vowel sound</u>.
e.g. *dŏg   mē   tīme   bōat   trāin*

Two syllable words have <u>two vowel sounds</u>.
e.g. *bācŏn   vĕlvĕt   năpkĭn   pīlŏt*

You can tell how many syllables are in a
word by counting the number of <u>vowel
sounds</u> you hear.

<u>Syllables may be closed.</u> Closed syllables
have short vowel sounds and end with one
or more consonants.
e.g. *ăt   bĕll   mĭlk   clŏck   hŭtch*

<u>Syllables may be open.</u> Open syllables end
with a single vowel that has a long sound.
e.g. *gō   bē   mȳ   flū   shē*

Syllables

A syllable consists of one or more letters, which must include at least one vowel, pronounced as one sound. It may be a word or part of a word.

e.g. **hăt** **bē'hāve** **brāin** **Brī'ăn**

REMEMBER:

The number of syllables is equal to the number of vowel sounds heard.

The letter _e_ at the end of a word is always silent and, as it has no sound, is not a syllable.

e.g.   **stôrę**   (1 syllable)

         stôry   (2 syllables)

Four Basic Types of Syllable

1. **Closed Syllables**.
   In a closed syllable one or more consonants follow the vowel. The vowel has its short sound and is marked with a breve.
   e.g. *ăt* *lĕg* *hĭll* *lŏdge* *hŭtch*

   Think of the vowel as a 'baby' vowel for it cannot say its name. The consonants that come after the vowel act as a gate closing in the 'baby' vowel and protecting it. Because the vowel is a baby, it has a cradle over it.
   căt - (ă) is a baby vowel, *t* is the gate.
   ĭn - (ĭ) is a baby vowel, *n* is the gate.

2. **Open Syllables**.
   A syllable is open if one vowel is at the end. That vowel has its long sound and is marked with a macron.
   e.g. *hē* *shē* *gō* *nō* *flū* *whȳ*

   There is no consonant closing in the vowel. The vowel stands alone, in the open, and it says its name. It is longing for protection so it is marked with a long line.

   mē *bē* *gō* *flū* *whȳ*

Four Basic Types of Syllable

3. **Open Accented Syllables.**
   In an open accented syllable the vowel
   sound is always long.

   e.g. $\bar{ba}$'con $\bar{e}$'ven $p\bar{i}$'lot
         $\bar{o}$'pen $\bar{u}$'niform

4. **Unaccented Syllables**
   An unaccented syllable is one in which
   e, o and u are half long.

   e.g. $d\acute{e}\,l\bar{e}te$ $h\acute{o}\,t\bar{e}l$ $h\acute{u}\,m\bar{a}ne$

   i and vowel y are always short.
   e.g. $d\breve{i}\,v\bar{i}de$ $c\breve{i}t\,\breve{y}$

   a is obscure and has the sound $(\breve{u})$.
   e.g. $ca\,n\breve{a}l$ $a\,l\breve{i}ke$

Spelling Vowel Sounds in Syllables.

A long vowel sound at the end of a
syllable is spelled with a single vowel.
e.g. *ā'corn,* *lē'gal,* *ī'ris,* *pō'ny,* *cū'pid*

1. *(ŭ)* in an accented syllable must be
   spelled *u*.
   e.g. *sŭl'len* *pŭp'pet*

2. *(ŭ)* in an unaccented syllable is usually
   spelled *a* (never *u*)
   e.g. *cŏm'mȧ (ŭ)* *lär'vȧ (ŭ)*

The sounds of *a*

1. At the end of an accented syllable, the
   sound is *(ā)* as in *ā'gent*.

2. In a closed syllable the sound is *(ă)* as
   in *bă̱t'on*.

3. At the end of an unaccented syllable,
   the sound is *(ŭ)* as in *cȧ năl'*.

Syllable Division Rules

V̆C'/CV   VC/CV̆'

When two consonants stand between two vowels, divide between the two consonants.

vccv
rabbit   *răb/bĭt*

vccv
arrest   *ăr/rĕst*

Which syllable is accented?

Determine the accent.

    răb'/bit ✓   *rab/bit'* ✗

    ăr'/rēst ✗   *ar/rest'* ✓

NOTE:
The vowel sound in an unaccented syllable changes its sound.

Syllable Division Rules

VCCV {Consonant Blends}

When two consonants stand between two vowels, syllable division usually occurs between the two consonants. Sometimes, the word contains a blend and the pattern is then VCCCV. However, a consonant blend sticks together in a syllable and acts as one consonant, The VCCV pattern can then be applied.

e.g.
    v c c c v   v c   c v

    wistful   *wist̲ / ful*

    v c c c v   v c   c v

    nostril   *nŏs / tril*

VCCV {Consonant Digraphs}

A consonant digraph sticks together in a syllable and acts as one consonant.

e.g.
    v c c c v   v c   c v

    bashful   *băsh̲ / ful*

    v c c c v   v c   c v

    anchor   *ăn / chor*

Syllable Division Rules

V'/CV {Regular Long Vowel Pattern}

When one consonant stands between two vowels, <u>the regular division is before the consonant</u>.

<u>vcv</u> *bacon*	*bā'con*	<u>vcv</u> *emit*	*ē'mit*
<u>vcv</u> *idol*	*ī'dol*	<u>vcv</u> *open*	*ō'pen*
<u>vcv</u> *unit*	*ū'nit*		

V̆C'/V {Irregular Short Vowel Pattern}

If the first vowel is short, <u>divide after the consonant</u>.

<u>vcv</u> *habit*	<u>*hăb*</u>*'it*	<u>vcv</u> *petal*	<u>*pĕt*</u>*'al*
<u>vcv</u> *linen*	<u>*lĭn*</u>*'en*	<u>vcv</u> *comic*	<u>*cŏm*</u>*'ic*
<u>vcv</u> *study*	<u>*stŭd*</u>*'y*		

Syllable Division Rules

V̟/CV'   e̲ o̲ u̲   in an unstressed first syllable.

In an open first syllable, which is unaccented, **e̲**, **o̲** and **u̲** are half-long. The long sound is simply held for a shorter length of time.

<u>vcv</u>
result   *re̟/sŭlt'*

<u>vcv</u>
hotel   *ho̟/tĕl'*

<u>vcv</u>
humane   *hu̟/māne'*

Syllable Division Rules

$\breve{V}/CV'$ *i* and vowel *y* at the end of an unaccented syllable.

At the end of an unaccented syllable, *i* and **vowel** *y* are always short.

$\overline{vcv}$
divide   *dĭ/vide'*

$\overline{vcv}$
city   *cĭt'/y*

REMEMBER

1. **Vowel** *y* takes the sound of *i*.

2. **Vowel** *y* takes the long sound of *i* (*ī*) in an accented syllable.
   e.g. ***cry, try, apply, reply, deny.***

3. **Vowel** *y* takes the short sound of *i* (*ĭ*) in an unaccented syllable but we often give the sound (*ē*) to the letter *y* when it comes at the end of words.
   e.g. ***penny   mummy   baby   pony***
   e is always silent at the end of words.

Syllable Division Rules

$\dot{V}/CV'$ __a__   in an unstressed syllable.

In an unaccented syllable, __a__ is obscure and has the sound *(ŭ)*.

    vcv
    canal   *cȧ/năl'*

    vcv
    alike   *ȧ/līke'*

REMEMBER

1. A vowel at the end of an unaccented syllable is long.

2. A vowel in a closed syllable is short.

3. At the end of an unaccented syllable:

   __e__   __o__ and   __u__   are half-long.
   __i__   and __vowel__ *y*   are always short.
   __a__   is obscure and sounds   *(ŭ)*.

Syllable Division Rules

VV   V/V

Occasionally, two vowels which usually form a digraph or a diphthong fall together and do not form the digraph or diphthong sound. **They must then divide**.

_oa_	**b<u>oa</u>t**	but	**bo/a**
_ue_	**d<u>ue</u>**	but	**du/et**
_oe_	**w<u>oe</u>**	but	**co/ed**
_ea_	**pr<u>ea</u>ch**	but	**cre/ate**
_ui_	**fr<u>ui</u>t**	but	**flu/id**
_ie_	**pr<u>ie</u>st**	but	**qui/et**
_oi_	**gr<u>oi</u>n**	but	**go/ing**

Part 4

Affixes

Suffixes

A suffix is a letter, or group of letters, added to the end of a baseword to change its use in a sentence.

e.g. Baseword - *run*

I *run*.
I am a *runner*.
I am *running*.
It is *runny*.

There are two kinds of suffix.

1. **Consonant suffixes** which begin with a consonant.

   e.g. *-s*   *-ful*   *-ness*   *-ly*

2. **Vowel suffixes** which begin with a vowel

   e.g. *-ing*   *-er*   *-able*   *-al*

REMEMBER:
A baseword is the simplest form of any English word to which suffixes may be added. When adding suffixes to basewords, always spell the baseword first then add the suffix.

Suffixes I have learned

Suffix	Meaning	v or c	Example
-s	*More than one thing*	c	*cats*
-ing	*act of, occurring in the present time.*	v	*talking*
-y	*full of; marked by*	v	*dusty*
-ed	*act which has occurred in the past*	v	*mended*
-less	*without*	c	*homeless*
-ful	*full of*	c	*cupful*
-ness	*quality of*	c	*sweetness*
-en	*made of; to make*	v	*golden*
-ly	*like*	c	*kingly*
-ly	*how*	c	*slowly*
-ly	*when*	c	*lately*
-ive	*inclined to*	v	*attractive*

Suffix Rule 1

Consonant Suffixes

A consonant suffix may be added to any baseword without changing the spelling of the baseword (providing it makes sense).

e.g.

king	+	*ship*	=	*kingship*
man	+	*ly*	=	*manly*
care	+	*less*	=	*careless*
play	+	*ful*	=	*playful*
wood	+	*s*	=	*woods*
forget	+	*ful*	=	*forgetful*
dry	+	*ness*	=	*dryness*

The following suffix rules (2 - 8) apply when adding vowel suffixes to basewords.

Suffix Rule 2

Basewords Ending VCC

A vowel suffix may be added to any baseword which ends in two consonants without changing the spelling of the baseword.

e.g.

$$jump + ing = \underline{jumping}$$

$$walk + ed = \underline{walked}$$

$$imp + ish = \underline{impish}$$

$$clang + er = \underline{clanger}$$

REMEMBER:

This links up with the short vowel pattern, VCCV.

e.g. *jumping,*   *impish*

Suffix Rule 3

<u>Basewords Ending   VVC</u>

A suffix can be added to any baseword which ends vowel - vowel - consonant (VVC) without changing the spelling of the baseword.

e.g.

$\overline{look}$ + *ing* =   <u>*looking*</u>

$\overline{read}$ + *er* =   <u>*reader*</u>

$\overline{weep}$ + *y* =   <u>*weepy*</u>

Suffix Rule 4

Words Ending in Vowel Digraphs & Diphthongs.

A suffix may be added to any baseword which ends in a vowel digraph or diphthong, without changing the spelling of the baseword.

e.g.

play +	*er*	=	*player*
snow +	*ing*	=	*snowing*
claw +	*ed*	=	*clawed*
boy +	*ish*	=	*boyish*

NOTE:
This rule does not apply to words ending in *ie* and *ue*. The Silent *e* Rule applies to words with these endings.

Suffix Rule 5

The Silent e Rule

Words ending in silent _**e**_ drop _**e**_ before a suffix beginning with a vowel, otherwise they do not.

e.g.   *hate* + *ing* = <u>*hating*</u>
   but
        hate + *ful* = <u>*hateful*</u>

REMEMBER:
This links up with the long vowel pattern <u>VCV</u>

e.g.   <u>VCV</u>   <u>VCV</u>
         hating   *hateful*

144

Exceptions to Silent e Rule

1. Words ending **_ce_** and **_ge_** keep the **_e_**
   before **_-able_** and **_-ous_** to preserve their
   soft sounds.
   e.g. **_changeable_**   **_serviceable_**   **_courageous_**

2. Keep the **_e_** to retain identity of
   word.

dye	*+ ing =*	*dyeing*	*- dying is a homophone*
singe	*+ ing =*	*singeing*	*- not singing*
hoe	*+ ing =*	*hoeing*	*- not hoing (oi)*
toe	*+ ing =*	*toeing*	*- not toing (oi)*
shoe	*+ ing =*	*shoeing*	*- not shoing (oi)*
canoe	*+ ing =*	*canoeing*	*- not canoing (oi)*
acre	*+ age=*	*acreage*	*- not acrage -*

   {a syllable would be lost if
   _e_ were dropped}

   There are others:
mile	*+ age=*	*mileage*	
fire	*+ y*	*= fiery*	

Exceptions to Silent e Rule

3. Some words that end in silent *e* drop the *e* before a consonant suffix.

   Truly, Mr. *Duly*, your *ninth* *argument* is *wholly* *awful* and that's the *truth*.
   also - *acknowledgment*; *judgment*

4. Two *i's* are unwise. Drop the *e* and change *i* to *y*.

   $$die + ing = dying$$
   $$lie + ing = lying$$
   $$tie + ing = tying$$
   $$vie + ing = vying$$

5. Three *e's* are not allowed.
   $$tree + ed = treed$$
   $$free + er = freer$$

Suffix Rule 6

The 1 - 1 - 1 Rule.

One syllable words, ending in one consonant after one vowel double the final consonant before a suffix beginning with a vowel.

e.g. $\underline{vc}$
         run
{1 syllable, 1 vowel,
{1 consonant after the vowel}

   run + ing = running

REMEMBER:
This links up with the short vowel pattern. VCCV

e.g. $\underline{vccv}$ $\underline{vccv}$ $\underline{vccv}$
         running   ***batted***   ***spotted***

NEVER DOUBLE ***x***

e.g.   ***tax + ing = taxing***
         box + er = boxer

x has the multiple consonant sound ***(ks)***

The 2 - 1 - 1 Rule.

Words of more than one syllable, ending in one consonant, after one vowel, double the final consonant before a vowel suffix IF the last syllable is accented.

e.g.
VC	VCCV
forge*t'*	-	*forgetting*
begi*n'*	-	*beginning*

but

| *o'*pen | - | *opening* |

IMPORTANT EXCEPTIONS

Words with the Latin root *fer* double *r* before *-ing* and *-ed* but should be checked before other suffixes.

e.g. *referring, referred* but *reference*.

REMEMBER

The last syllable of a 2-1-1 word is treated like a 1-1-1 word when it is accented.

Suffix Rule 8

Final Y Rule

1. Words ending in *y* after a <u>consonant</u> change *y* to *i* before any suffix. {unless the suffix begins with *i*} {because <u>two *i*'s are unwise</u>}

   e.g. *fr̊y* - *fried* but *frying*

   cr̊y - *cried* but *crying*

2. Words ending in *y* <u>after a vowel</u> are unchanged before any suffix.

   e.g. *bo̊y + ish* = *boyish*

   påy + ment = *payment*

3. The following words retain *y* before *ly* and *ness*.

   shy   *wry*   *spry*   *dry*

   e.g. *dry - drier, driest* but *dryly* and *dryness*

Prefixes

Prefix	Meaning	Keyword	Origin
ab	*from*	*absence*	*(Latin)*
ante	*before*	*anteroom*	"
anti	*against*	*antifreeze*	"
dis	*opposite of*	*disappear*	"
ex	*out of*	*export*	"
il	*not*	*illegal*	"
im	*not*	*impossible*	"
in	*not*	*inefficient*	"
inter	*between*	*interchange*	"
ir	*not*	*irregular*	"
pre	*before*	*prehistoric*	"
pro	*infront of*	*project*	"
re	*again*	*return*	"
semi	*half*	*semicircle*	"
sub	*under*	*subnormal*	"
trans	*across*	*transfer*	"
en	*into*	*entangle*	*(Anglo Saxon)*
mis	*wrong, wrongly*	*misbehave*	"
over	*over*	*overgrown*	"
un	*not*	*uncovered*	"
under	*under*	*underground*	"

Prefixes

A prefix is a syllable that is put at the beginning of a baseword and so changes the meaning of the word.

When a prefix is added to a baseword, the spelling of the baseword does not change.

e.g. **un*wise*** **mis*deed*** **dis*array***

When the last letter of the prefix is the same as the first letter of the baseword, a double consonant occurs.

e.g. **mis*spent*** **un*necessary*** **dis*service***

Prefixes are accented in nouns.

e.g. **<u>rĕf'</u>/use** **<u>prŏ'</u>/ject**

Prefixes are not accented in verbs.

e.g. **rĕ/fuse'** **prŏ/ject'**

Part 5

Plurals and Possesives

Nouns: Singular and Plural

A **noun** is the name of:

a <u>person</u>,   John,   Mary,   Mr.Jones
a <u>place</u>,   London, Liverpool, Surrey
a <u>thing</u>,   book, table, boy, girl, cat

A singular noun means <u>only one thing</u>.
e.g.   a ***pin***,   one ***toy***,   a ***park***.

A <u>plural noun</u> means <u>more than one thing</u>.
e.g.   two ***pins***,   many ***toys***,   some ***parks***.

To make a singular noun plural, we usually
just add <u>s</u>.

<u>Singular</u>   <u>Plural</u>

one ***lad***   two ***lads***
a ***girl***   many ***girls***
one ***bird***   ten ***birds***
a ***desk***   some ***desks***

154

Plural Rule: Adding <u>s</u>

The regular plural of a noun (a naming word) is spelled by adding <u>**s**</u> to the singular noun.

e.g. <u>Singular noun</u> <u>Plural noun</u>
       one ***cat***   ten ***cats***
       a ***dog***   many ***dogs***

<u>Third person singular verbs add</u> <u>**s**</u>

1. This means that <u>**s**</u> is added to a verb (a doing word) after ***he***, ***she*** and ***it***.

   e.g. He ***runs***. She ***tells***. It ***grows***.

2. <u>**s**</u> is also added to a verb after <u>the name of one person</u> or <u>one thing</u>.

   e.g. ***Tim rides<u>.</u>*** ***The cat jumps<u>.</u>***

Plural Rule: Adding es

Words ending in a sibilant sound, (a hissing sound) add **es** to form the plural. You can hear the extra syllable. The sibilant endings are **s (s), x, z, ch** and **sh**.

e.g.

bus	*buses*
box	*boxes*
buzz	*buzzes*
church	*churches*
fish	*fishes.*

Third person singular verbs follow the same rule.

e.g.
He passes
Bill taxes his car
The bee buzzes
It matches
The girl wishes

REMEMBER:
A noun is a naming word.
A verb is a doing word.

Plural Rule: Final y

1. Words ending in **y** <u>after a consonant</u> form the plural by changing **y** to **i** and adding **es**.

   e.g. *lady*   *<u>ladies</u>*

        penny   *<u>pennies</u>*.

---

2. Words ending in **y** <u>after a vowel</u> just add **s**.

   e.g. *boy*   *<u>boys</u>*

        play   *<u>plays</u>*

---

3. Third person singular verbs follow the same rule.

   e.g. *He tries*
   She carries
   It worries
   Tom employs
   Lucy displays

Plural Rule: Final __f__   __fe__

1. Most words ending in __*f*__ or __*fe*__ form .
    the plurals by adding __s__.
    e.g. __*muffs*__   __*roofs*__   __*cafes*__   __*beliefs*__

2. The following 13 words <u>MUST</u> change __*f*__
    to __*v*__ and add __*es*__. Learn them.

elf	-	*elves*	*thief* -	*thieves*
self	-	*selves*	*leaf* -	*leaves*
shelf	-	*shelves*	*sheaf* -	*sheaves*
life	-	*lives*	*half* -	*halves*
wife	-	*wives*	*calf* -	*calves*
knife	-	*knives*	*loaf* -	*loaves*
wolf	-	*wolves*		

LOOK OUT FOR VERBS (doing words)
e.g.
He __*believes*__ in mercy. (VERB)
My __*beliefs*__ are known. (NOUN)

She __*grieves*__ for her father. (VERB)
He carries the __*griefs*__ of the world. (NOUN)

Plural Rule: Final o

1. Words ending in **o** after a vowel add **s** to form the plural.

   e.g. **radios** **patios** **kangaroos** **rodeos**

2. Words ending in **o** after a consonant add **es** to form the plural.

   e.g. **echoes** **tomatoes** **heroes** **potatoes**

EXCEPTIONS:

Musical terms of Italian origin.
   piano - pianos
   alto - altos.

Words of Spanish origin.
   poncho - ponchos
   burro - burros.

Common Irregular Plurals

ox	oxen
policeman	policemen
mouse	mice
woman	women
foot	feet
gentleman	gentlemen
tooth	teeth
deer	deer
goose	geese
sheep	sheep
louse	lice
moose	moose
child	children
grouse	grouse
man	men
swine	swine

Possessive Rules

1. To make <u>Singular Possessives</u>
   add **'s**.
   e.g. the ***boy's*** cap; the ***girl's*** coat.

2. To make <u>Plural Possessives</u>

    i)   Make the word plural.
    ii) Lift pencil from paper.
    iii) Add apostrophe.
    iv) Add **s** ONLY if plural doesn't
         end in **s**.

   e.g.

Word	***boy***	***man***	***lady***	***child***
Make Plural	***boys***	***men***	***ladies***	***children***
Lift Pencil	*(think about the word)*			
Add Apostrophe	***boys'***	***men'***	***ladies'***	***children'***
Add **s** if necessary	**-**	***men's***	**-**	***children's***

3. Proper nouns follow the same rules.
   e.g. ***Mr. Jones's car***
        the Joneses' car

   BUT men of fame may use just the
   apostrophe.
   e.g. ***Dickens'*** novels.

Possessive Rules

4. Indefinite pronouns are always singular possessive.

   e.g. *everyone's luck*   *everybody's luck*
   anyone's chance   *anybody's chance*
   someone's life   *somebody's life*
   no one's wish   *nobody's wish.*

5. Possessive pronouns NEVER use an apostrophe.

   yours   ours   his   hers
   theirs   its   whose

   e.g. *This house is ours.*

   NOTE:
   its is a pronoun; *it's* means it is.
   whose is a pronoun; *who's* means who is.

6. Plurals of letters, figures and signs are formed by adding *'s*.   e.g.

   Dot your i's and cross your t's.
   Mind your p's and q's.
   Put +'s on the left and -'s on the right.

   Without the apostrophe, there would be confusion with words.

Part 6

Other

Parts of Speech

Noun

Noun - the name of a person, a place or a thing.

e.g. ***Jack   Betty   London   the desk   a cat***

Verb

Verb - a doing or action word

e.g. ***to run, to talk, to write, to learn.***

Remember: ***to be*** *(am, is, are, was, were).*

to have *(have, has, had).*

Adjective

Adjective - a describing word - tells you more about a noun.

e.g. ***a big cat,   a dark night.***

Adverb

Adverb - tells you how, when, or where an action takes place.

I walk slowly. (How do I walk?)

He came early. (When did he come?)

She creeps forward. (Where did she creep?)

Tells you what a person/thing is like.

He was friendly. (What was he like?)

164

Third Person Singular Verbs

1st   Person speaking or writing
        is **1st Person.**

2nd   Person spoken to, or written to,
        is the **2nd Person.**

3rd   Person spoken of, or written about,
        is the **3rd Person**

1st Person Singular =   **I**
2nd Person Singular =   **You**
3rd Person Singular =   **He**, **She**, **It** or
    the name of one person or one thing.

Third Person Singular verbs add **s**.
That means that **s** is added to a verb (a
doing word) after **he**, **she** and **it**.

e.g.   *He runs* but *they run.*
            She swims but *we swim.*
            It grows but *I grow.*

s is also added to a verb after the name
of one person or one thing.

e.g. *I ride on the bus and Tom rides too.*
     We jump over the wall and the cat jumps.

Blends

Two or more adjacent letters whose sounds flow smoothly together.

Initial Blends

L Blends
bl,   cl,   fl,   gl,   pl,   sl,   spl

R Blends
*br,   cr,   dr,   fr,   gr,   pr,   spr,
str,   scr,   shr,   tr,   thr*

S Blends
*sc,   sl,   sm,   sn,   sp,   st,   sk,
scr,   spr,   str,   squ,   sw*

W Blends
dw,   sw,   tw

Final Blends

L Blends
-ld,   -lf,   -lp,   -lt,   -lk

M and N Blends
-mp,   -nd,   -nk,   -ng,   -nt

S Blends
-sp,   -st,   -sk,

Others
-ft,   -ct,   -pt

Short Vowel Spellings

Vowel	*Begin*	*Middle*	*Ending*
(ă)	*a*	*a*	*English words do not end in this sound*
(ĕ)	*e*	*e*	*English words do not end in this sound*
(ĕ)		*ea*	*English words do not end in this sound*
(ĭ)	*i*	*i*	*English words do not end in the letter i*
(ĭ)		*y*	*y*
(ŏ)	*o*	*o*	*English words do not end in this sound*
(ŏ)		*w wh qu a*	*English words do not end in this sound*
(ŭ)	*u*	*u*	
(ŭ)	*a*	*a*	*a*
(ŭ)	*o*	*o*	
(ŭ)		*ou*	
(ŭ)		*e*	
(o͝o)		*oo*	
(o͝o)		*u*	

REMEMBER:

The sound ***(ŭ)*** is regularly spelled ***u*** in a stressed syllable and ***a*** in an unstressed syllable.

Long Vowel Spellings

vowel sound	open syllables	choices in order of frequency in main syallables	word endings	other endings in longer words
(ā)	a	a - e	ay	a - e
(ā)		ai		
(ā)		ei	ey	
(ā)		eigh	eigh	
(ā)		ea		
(ē)	e	ee	ee	e - e
(ē)		ea	ey	
(ē)		ie		
(ē)		c - ei		
(ē)		e - e		
(ī)	i	i - e	y	i - e
(ī)		igh	ie	
(ī)		y - e	igh	
(ō)	o	o - e	ow	o - e
(ō)		oa	oe	
(ō)		ow		
(ū)	u	u - e	ue	u - e
(ū)		eu	ew	
(o͞o)		oo		
(o͞o)		ou		
(o͞o)		ui		

REMEMBER:

In an open syllable the long vowel sound
is always spelled with a single vowel.

Index

Index

Phonetical Index

Diacritical Markings

The diacritical markings are the distinguishing marks which indicate the pronounciation for which a letter or combination of letters stand.

1. *(˘)* Breve - indicates short vowel. *(ă)* as in **apple**

2. *(⁻)* Macron - indicates a long vowel *(ā)* as in **acorn**

3. *(â)* Modified Macron - indicates half long vowel
   (ė) as in **elect**

4. *(^)* Circumflex - indicates the stressed sound of <u>o</u> and <u>u</u> when modified by <u>r</u>.
   (ôr) as in **horn** *(ûr)* as in **burn**

5. *(˜)* Tilde - indicates the unstressed sound of vowels modified by <u>r</u>
   (ẽr) as in **teacher**

6. *(ä)* Broad <u>a</u> sounding like *(är)* as in **path**.

7. *(ă)* Obscure <u>a</u> sounding like *(ŭ)* as in **panda**, **parade**

The above list is for completeness.
The breve *(˘)* and macron *(⁻)* will definitely be needed, but it may not be necessary for students to be aware of the other diacritical markings.